Corporate Culture and the Attack on Higher Education and Public Schooling

by
Henry A. Giroux

ISBN 0-87367-642-4
Copyright © 1999 by the Phi Delta Kappa Educational Foundation
Bloomington, Indiana

This fastback is sponsored by the
Ohio State University Chapter of
Phi Delta Kappa International, which
made a generous contribution toward
publication costs.

The chapter sponsors this fastback
to honor Martha Wilson Alcock.
Her service and leadership have been
instrumental in the fellowship,
maintenance, and growth of the chapter.

Table of Contents

The Final Victory of Liberal Democracy?....... 7

Politics, Power, and Corporate Culture......... 12

Education and the Rise of the
   Corporate Manager........................ 16

Corporate Culture as a Model of Leadership ... 23

Privatizing and Commercializing
   Public Schools 29

Education and the Imperatives of Democracy .. 42

Notes 48

Democracy has failed because so many people fear it. They believe that wealth and happiness are so limited that a world full of intelligent, healthy, and free people is impossible, if not undesirable. . . . Such a world, with all its contradictions, can be saved, can yet be born again; but not out of capital, interest, property, and gold.[1]

The Final Victory of Liberal Democracy?

A recent full-page advertisement for *Forbes 500 Magazine* proclaims in bold red letters, "Capitalists of the World Unite."[2] Beneath the slogan, covering the bottom half of the page, is a mass of individuals, representing various countries throughout the world, their arms raised in victory. Instead of workers in the traditional sense, the *Forbes* professionals (three women in all) are distinctly middle class, dressed in sport jackets, ties, carrying brief cases or cellular phones. A sea of red flags with their respective national currency emblazoned on the front of each waves above their heads. At the bottom of the picture is a text that reads, "All hail the final victory of capitalism." At first glance, the ad appears to be simply a mockery of one of Marxism's most powerful ideals. But as self-conscious as the ad is in parodying the dream of a workers' revolution, it also reflects another ideology made famous in 1989 by Francis Fukuyama, who proclaimed "the end of history,"[3] a reference to the end of authoritarian communism in East Central Europe, the former Soviet Union, and the Baltic countries. According to Fukuyama, "the end of history" meant that liberal democracy has achieved its ultimate victory and that the twin ideologies of the market and representative democracy now constitute, with a few exceptions, the universal values of the new global village.

The *Forbes* ad does more than signal the alleged "death" of communism, it also cancels out the tension between market values and those values representative of civil society that cannot be measured in strictly commercial terms but are critical to democracy. I am referring specifically to values such as justice, freedom, equality, health and respect for children, the rights of citizens as equal and free human beings, as well as "respect for the rule of law, for individual rights for value pluralism, for constitutional guarantees. . . and democratic politics."[4]

Who are the cheering men (and three women) portrayed in this ad? Certainly not the 43 million Americans who have lost their jobs in the last 15 years. Certainly not "the people." The *Forbes* ad celebrates freedom, but only in the discourse of the unbridled power of the market. There is no recognition here (how could there be?) of either the limits that democracies must place on such power or how corporate culture and its narrow redefinition of freedom as a private good may actually present a threat to democracy equal to, if not greater than, that imagined under communism or any other totalitarian ideology.

Fukuyama, of course, proved to be right about the fall of communism but quite wrong about "the universalization of Western liberal democracy as the final form of government."⁵ Before the ink was dry on his triumphalist proclamation, ethnic genocide erupted in Bosnia Herzegovina, Moslem fundamentalism swept Algeria, the Russians launched a blood bath in Chechnya, and parts of Africa erupted in a bloody civil war accompanied by the horror of tribal genocide. Even in the United States, with the Cold War at an end, the language of democracy seemed to lose its vitality and purpose as an organizing principle for society. As corporations have gained more and more power in American society, democratic culture becomes corporate culture, the rightful ideological heir to the victory over socialism.⁶

I use the term *corporate culture* to refer to an ensemble of ideological and institutional forces that functions politically and pedagogically to both govern organizational life through senior managerial control and to produce compliant workers, spectorial consumers, and passive citizens.⁷ Within the language and images of corporate culture, citizenship is portrayed as an utterly privatized affair whose aim is to produce competitive self-interested individuals vying for their own material and ideological gain. Reformulating social issues as strictly individual or economic issues, corporate culture functions largely to cancel out the democratic impulses and practices of civil society by either devaluing them or absorbing such impulses within a market logic. No longer a space for political struggle, culture in the corporate model becomes an all-encompassing horizon for producing market identities, values, and practices. The good life, in this discourse, "is construed in terms of our identities as consumers — we are what we buy."⁸ Public spheres are replaced by commercial spheres as the substance of critical democracy is emptied out and replaced by a democracy of goods, consumer lifestyles, shopping malls, and the increasing expansion of the cultural and political power of corporations throughout the world.

The broader knowledge, social values, and skills necessary for creating substantive democratic participation increasingly seem at odds with and detrimental to corporate moguls, such as Bill Gates, the new cultural heroes and icons of social mobility, wealth, and success. Within the world of national politics, conservative policy institutes along with a Republican Congress incessantly argue that how we think about education, work, and social welfare means substituting the language of the private good for the discourse and values of the public good. At the economic level, the ascendancy of corporate culture has become evident in the growing power of mega-conglomerates, such as Disney, General Electric, Time-Warner, and Westinghouse, to control both the content and distribution of much of what the American public sees.[9]

Accountable only to the bottom line of profitability, corporate culture and its growing influence in American life has signaled a radical shift in both the notion of public culture and what constitutes the meaning of citizenship and the defense of the public good. For example, the rapid resurgence of corporate power in the last 20 years and the attendant reorientation of culture to the demands of commerce and regulation have substituted the language of personal responsibility and private initiative for the discourses of social responsibility and public service. This can be seen in government policies designed to dismantle state protections for the poor, the environment, working people, and people of color.[10] For example, the 1996 welfare law signed by President Clinton reduces food stamp assistance for millions of children in working families; and a study by the Urban Institute showed that the bill would move 2.6 million people, including 1.1 million children, into poverty.[11] Other examples include the dismantling of race-based programs, such as the "California Civil Rights Initiative" and the landmark affirmative-action case, *Hopwood* v. *Texas*, both designed to eliminate affirmative action in higher education; the reduction of federal monies for urban development, such as HUD's housing program; and a massive increase in many state funds spent on corrections at the expense of funding for public higher education.[12]

As a result of the corporate takeover of public life, the maintenance of democratic public spheres from which to organize the energies of a moral vision loses all relevance. As the power of civil society is reduced in its ability to impose or make corporate power accountable, politics as an expression of democratic struggle is deflated, and it becomes more difficult within the logic of self-help and the bottom line to address pressing social and moral issue in systemic and political terms. This suggests a dangerous turn in American society, one that threatens both our understanding of democracy as fundamental to our freedom and the ways in which we address the meaning and purpose of education.

Politics, Power, and Corporate Culture

Politics is the performative register of moral action; it is the mark of a civilized society to prevent justice from going dead in each of us; it is a call to acknowledge the claims of humanity to eliminate needless suffering while affirming freedom, equality, and hope. Markets do not reward moral behavior; and as corporate culture begins to dominate public life, it becomes more difficult for citizens to think critically and act morally. For instance, what opportunities exist within the logic of privatization and excessive individualism for citizens to protest the willingness of the United States Congress to serve the needs of corporate interests over pressing social demands? I am not referring simply to the power of individuals and groups to limit government subsidies and bailouts that benefit corporate interests, but to curtail those forms of institutional insanity that have severe consequences for the most vulnerable of our citizens — the young, aged, and the poor. For example, with no countervailing powers, norms, or values in place in civil society to counter corporate power, how can the average citizen protest and stop the willingness of Congress to fund B2 Stealth bombers at a cost of $2 billion each while refusing to allocate $100 million to expand child nutrition programs? This is a political and moral default that appears all the more shameful given the fact that 26% of children in the United States live below the poverty line.[13] In a society increasingly governed by profit considerations and the logic of the market, where is the critical language to be developed, nourished, and applied for prioritizing public over private democracy, the social good over these market forces that benefit a very small group of investors, or social justice over rampant greed and individualism?

As the rise of corporate culture reasserts the primacy of privatization and individualism, there is an increasing call for people to surrender or narrow their capacities for engaged politics for a market-based notion of identity, one that suggests relinquishing our roles as social subjects for the limited role of consuming subjects. Similarly, as corporate culture extends ever deeper into the basic institutions of civil and political society, there is a simultaneous diminishing of non-commodified public spheres — those institutions engaged in dialogue, education, and learning that address the relationship of the self to public life, social responsibility to the broader demands of citizenship, and the development of public spheres that invest public culture with vibrancy.

History has been clear about the dangers of unbridled corporate power.[14] The brutal practices of slavery, the exploitation of child labor, the sanctioning of the cruelest working conditions in the mines and sweatshops of America and abroad, and the destruction of the environment have all been fueled by the law of maximizing profits and minimizing costs, especially when there has been no countervailing power from civil society to hold such powers in check. This is not to suggest that capitalism is the enemy of democracy, but that in the absence of a strong civil society and the imperatives of a strong democratic public sphere, the power of corporate culture when left on its own appears to respect few boundaries based on self-restraint and those non-commodified, broader human values that are central to a democratic civic culture. John Dewey was right in arguing that democracy requires work, but that work is not synonymous with democracy.[15]

Struggling for democracy is both a political and educational task. Fundamental to the rise of a vibrant democratic culture is the recognition that education must be treated as a public good and not merely as a site for commercial investment or for affirming a notion of the private good based exclusively on the fulfillment of individual needs. Reducing higher and public education to the status of a handmaiden of corporate culture works against the critical social imperative of educating citizens who can sustain and develop inclusive democratic public spheres. There is a long tradition extending from Thomas Jefferson to C. Wright Mills that extols the importance of education as essential for a democratic public life. This legacy of public discourse appears to have faded as education consultants all over America, from Robert Zemsky of Stanford to Chester Finn of the

Hudson Institute, now call for education institutions to "advise their clients in the name of efficiency to act like corporations selling products and seek 'market niches' to save themselves" and meet the challenges of the New World Order.[16]

In what follows, I want to address the fundamental shift in society regarding how we think about the relationship between corporate culture and democracy.[17] Specifically, I want to argue that one of the most important indications of such a change can be seen in the ways in which we are currently being asked to rethink the role of higher education and public education. Underlying this analysis is the assumption that the struggle to reclaim the public schools and higher education must be seen as part of a broader battle over the defense of the public good, and that at the heart of such a struggle is the need to challenge the ever-growing discourse and influence of corporate culture, power, and politics. I will conclude by offering some suggestions as to what educators can do to address this problem in order to reassert the primacy of higher and public education as essential spheres for expanding and deepening the processes of democracy and civil society.

Education and the Rise of the Corporate Manager

In a recent issue of *The Chronicle of Higher Education*, Katherine S. Mangan reported that there is a growing number of presidential searches "looking for leaders who can bridge business and academe."[18] According to Mangan, this has resulted in a large number of business-school deans being offered jobs as college or university presidents. The rationale for such actions appears to be that "Business deans are often in a strong position to cultivate corporate contacts. . . . [and are] better at translating the academic environment to the outside world."[19] Mangan's article makes clear that what was once part of the hidden curriculum of higher education — the creeping vocationalization and subordination of learning to the dictates of the market — has become an open and defining principle of education at all levels of learning.

According to Stanley Aronowitz, many colleges and universities are experiencing financial hard times brought on by the end of the Cold War and the dwindling of government-financed defense projects, coupled with a sharp reduction of state aid to higher education. As a result, they are all too happy to allow corporate leaders to run their institutions, form business partnerships, establish cushy relationships with business-oriented legislators, and develop curricula tailored to the needs of corporate interests.[20] In some cases this has meant that universities, such as the Massachusetts Institute of Technology and the University of California at Irvine, have cut deals with corporations by offering to do product research and cede to their corporate backers the patents for such inventions and discoveries in return for ample research money.

Further evidence of the vocationalization of higher education can be found in the increasing willingness on the part of legislators, government representatives, and school officials to rely on corporate leaders to establish the terms of the debate in the media regarding the meaning and purpose of higher and public education. One typical example can be found in the highly publicized pronouncements of Louis Gerstner Jr., who is the Chairman and CEO of IBM. In an editorial in *USA Today*, Gerstner argues that schools should be treated like businesses because when "U.S. businesses were faced with a stark choice: change or close. They changed. They began to invest in substantial transformation, new methods of production, new kinds of worker training. Most importantly, they continually benchmarked performance against one another and against international competition. . . . And it worked."[21] For Gerstner and many other CEOs, the current success of the capitalist economy is the direct result of the leadership exercised by corporate America. The lesson to be drawn is simple: "Schools are oddly insulated from marketplace forces and the discipline that drives constant adaptation, self-renewal and a relentless push for excellence."[22] Gerstner's argument is instructive because it is so typical, primarily about issues of efficiency, accountability, and restructuring. Corporate organizations, such as the Committee for Economic Development, an organization of executives at about 250 corporations, have been more blunt about their interest in education. Not only has the group argued that social goals and services get in the way of learning basic skills but also that many employers in the business community feel dissatisfied because "a large majority of their new hires lack adequate writing and problem-solving skills."[23]

Given the narrow nature of corporate concerns, it is not surprising that when matters of accountability become part of the language of school reform, they are divorced from broader considerations of ethics, equity, and justice. This type of corporate discourse not only lacks a vision beyond its own pragmatic interests, it also lacks a self-critical inventory about its own ideology and its effects on society. But, of course, one would not expect such concerns to emerge within corporations, where questions of consequence begin and end with the bottom line. Questions about the effects of downsizing, de-industrialization, and the "trend toward more low-paid, temporary, benefit-free, blue- and white-collar jobs and fewer decent permanent factory and office jobs"[24] caused by the reforms implemented by such companies as IBM must come from those democratic arenas that business seeks to "restructure." Megacorporations will say nothing about their profound role in promoting the flight of capital abroad; the widening gap between intellectual, technical, and manual labor and the growing class of permanently underemployed in a mass of "deskilled" jobs; the growing inequality between the rich and the poor; or the scandalous use of child labor in Third World countries. The onus of responsibility is placed on educated citizens to recognize that corporate principles of efficiency, accountability, and profit maximization have not created new jobs but in most cases have eliminated them.[25] My point, of course, is that such absences in public discourse constitute a defining principle of corporate discourse, which refuses to address — and must be made to address — the scarcity of moral vision that inspires such calls for school reform modeled after corporate reforms implemented in the last decade.

But the modeling of higher education after corporate principles and the partnerships they create with the business community do more than reorient the purpose and meaning of higher education; such reforms also instrumentalize the curricula and narrow what it means to extend knowledge to broader social concerns. Business-university partnerships provide just one concrete example of the willingness of both educators and corporate executives to acknowledge the effects such mergers have on the production and dissemination of knowledge in the interest of the public good. Lost in the willingness of such schools as MIT to sell part of their curricula to the corporations is the ethical consequence of ignoring basic science research that benefits humanity as a whole, because such research offers little as a profit-maximizing venture. Ralph Nader recently indicated in a nationally broadcast speech on C-Span that one result of such transactions is that the universities are doing far too little to develop anti-malaria and tuberculosis vaccines at a time when these diseases are once again killing large numbers of people in Third World countries; such interventions are viewed as unprofitable investments.[26] Research guided only by the controlling yardstick of profit undermines the role of the university as a public sphere dedicated to addressing the most serious social problems a society faces. Moreover, the corporate model of research instrumentalizes knowledge and undermines forms of theorizing, pedagogy, and meaning that define higher and public education as a public good rather than as a private good.

Missing from much of the corporate discourse on schooling is any analysis of how power works in shaping knowledge, how the teaching of broader social values provides safeguards against turning citizen skills into simply training skills for the workplace, or how schooling can help students reconcile the seemingly opposing needs of freedom and solidarity in order to forge a new conception of civic courage and democratic public life. Knowledge as capital in the corporate model is privileged as a form of investment in the economy but appears to have little value when linked to the power of self-definition and social responsibility or to the capacities of individuals to expand the scope of freedom, justice, and the operations of democracy.[27] Knowledge stripped of ethical and political considerations offers limited, if any, insights into how schools should educate students to push against the oppressive boundaries of gender, class, race, and age domination. Nor does such a language provide the pedagogical conditions for students to critically engage knowledge as an ideology deeply implicated in issues and struggles concerning the production of identities, culture, power, and history. Education is a moral and political practice and always presupposes an introduction to and preparation for particular forms of social life, a particular rendering of what community is, and what the future might hold.

If pedagogy is, in part, about the production of identities, then curricula modeled after corporate culture have been enormously successful in preparing students for low-skilled, service work in a society that has little to offer in the way of meaningful employment for the vast majority of its graduates. If CEOs are going to provide some insight into how education should be reformed, they will have to reverse their tendency to collapse the boundaries between corporate culture and civic culture, between a society that defines itself through the interests of corporate power and one that defines itself through more democratic considerations regarding what constitutes substantive citizenship and social responsibility. Moreover, they will have to recognize that the problems with American schools cannot be reduced to matters of accountability or cost-effectiveness. Nor can the solutions to such problems be reduced to the spheres of management and economics. The problems of higher education and public schooling must be addressed in the realms of values and politics, while engaging critically the most fundamental beliefs Americans have as a nation regarding the meaning and purpose of education and its relationship to democracy.

Corporate Culture as a Model of Leadership

As universities increasingly model themselves after corporations, it becomes crucial to understand how the principles of corporate culture intersect with the meaning and purpose of the university, the role of knowledge production for the 21st century, and the social practices inscribed within teacher-student relationships. The signs are not encouraging.

In many ways, the cost-accounting principles of efficiency, calculability, predictability, and control of the corporate order have restructured the meaning and purpose of education. As I have mentioned previously, many deans are now given the title of CEO, academic programs are streamlined to cut costs, and in many colleges new presidents are actively pursuing ways to establish closer ties between their respective colleges and the business community. For example, the *New York Times* reports, in what has become a typical story, that a business-oriented president at George Mason University has emphasized technology training in order to "boost the university's financing (by the state legislature) by as much as $25 million a year, provided that George Mason cultivates stronger ties with northern Virginia's booming technology industry."[28]

In other quarters in higher education, the results of the emergence of the corporate university appear even more ominous. James Carlin, a multimillionaire and successful insurance executive who now serves as chairman of the Massachusetts State Board of Education, recently gave a speech to the Greater Boston Chamber of Commerce. In a statement that betrays his ignorance of the recent history and commission of higher education, Carlin argued that colleges need to be downsized just as businesses have been in the past decade, that tenure should be abolished, and that faculty have too much power in shaping decisions in the university. Carlin's conclusion: "At least 50% of all non-hard sciences research on American campuses is a lot of foolishness" and should be banned.[29] Pointing to the rising costs of higher education, he further predicted that "there's going to be a revolution in higher education. Whether you like it or not, it's going to be broken apart and put back together differently. It won't be the same. Why should it be? Why should everything change except for higher education?"[30] Carlin's "revolution" has been spelled out in his call for increasing the workload of professors to four 3-credit courses a semester, effectively reducing the time such educators might have for doing research or shaping institutional power.

There is more at stake in university reform than the realities and harsh principles of cost-cutting. Corporate culture in its reincarnation in the 1980s and 1990s appears to have little patience with non-commodified knowledge or with the more lofty ideals that have defined higher education as a public service. Carlin's anti-intellectualism and animosity toward educators and students alike signal that, as higher education comes under the influence of corporate ideologies, universities will be largely refashioned in the image of the new multiconglomerate landscape. One consequence will be an attempt to curtail academic freedom and tenure. As one business-oriented administrator admitted in a conversation about tenure to Bill Tierney, "We have to focus on the priorities of the. . . school and not the individual. We must industrialize the school, and tenure — academic freedom — isn't part of that model."[31] Missing from this model of leadership is the recognition that academic freedom implies that knowledge has a critical function, that intellectual inquiry that is unpopular and critical should be safeguarded and treated as an important social asset, and that public intellectuals are more than mere functionaries of the corporate order. Such ideals are at odds with the vocational function that corporate culture wants to assign to higher education.

While the appeal to downsizing higher education appears to have caught the public's imagination at the moment, the fact is that such "reorganization" has been going on for some time. Indeed, more professors are working part time and at two-year community colleges than at any other time in the country's recent history. Alison Schneider recently pointed out in the *Chronicle of Higher Education* that "in 1970, only 22% of the professorate worked part time. By 1995, that proportion had nearly doubled to 41%."[32] Creating a permanent underclass of part-time professional workers in higher education is not only demoralizing and exploitative for many faculty who inhabit such jobs. Such policies increasingly deskill both part- and full-time faculty by increasing the amount of work they have to do, while simultaneously shifting power away from the faculty to the managerial sectors of the university. Corporate culture has invested heavily in leadership from the top as evidenced by the huge salaries many CEOs get. Chrysler chief, Robert Eaton, earned $11.3 million in 1997, while Michael Eisner, the CEO of Walt Disney Inc., is estimated to have received over $1 billion since he arrived at Disney 14 years ago.[33] But the price to pay for such a model of leadership appears to undermine even the weakest image of the university as a public space for creating democratic values, critical teaching communities, and equitable work relations.

Held up to the profit standard, universities and colleges will increasingly calibrate supply to demand, and the results look ominous with regard to what forms of knowledge and research will be rewarded and legitimated. In addition, it appears that populations marked by class and racial subordination will have less access to higher education. As globalization and corporate mergers increase, technologies develop, and cost-effective practices expand, there will be fewer jobs for certain professionals resulting in the inevitable elevation of admission standards, restriction of student loans, and the reduction of student access to higher education.

Stanley Aronowitz argues that the changing nature of intellectual labor, knowledge production, and the emerging glut of professionals on a global scale undermines mass education as the answer to the growing underemployment of the professional classes. He writes:

> Although the media hypes that millions of new jobs require specialized, advanced knowledge and credentials, the bare truth is that technological change, globalization, and relatively slow growth have reduced the demand for certain professionals. . . . And despite the boom of the middle 1990s, chronic shortages of physicians, accountants and attorneys have all but disappeared. In fact, the globalization of intellectual labor is beginning to affect knowledge industries, with Indian and Chinese engineers and computer designers performing work that was once almost exclusively done in North America and western Europe. And do nonscientists really need credentials signifying they have completed a prescribed program to perform most intellectual labor? If jobs are the intended outcome of a credential, there are few arguments for mass higher education. [34]

Fewer jobs in higher education means fewer students will be enrolled or have access, but it also means that the processes of vocationalization — fueled by corporate values that mimic "flexibility," "competition," or "lean production," and rationalized through the application of accounting principles — poses the threat of gutting many academic departments and programs that cannot translate their subject matter into commercial gains. Programs and courses that focus on such areas as critical theory, literature, feminism, ethics, environmentalism, post-colonialism, philosophy, and sociology suggest an intellectual cosmopolitanism or a concern with social issues that will be either eliminated or technicized because their role in the market will be judged as ornamental. Similarly, those working conditions that allow professors and graduate assistants to comment extensively on student work, provide small seminars for classes, spend time with student advising, conduct independent studies, and do collaborative research with both faculty colleagues and students do not appear consistent with the imperatives of downsizing, efficiency, and cost-accounting.[35]

Privatizing and Commercializing Public Schools

The corporatizing of public education has taken a different but no less ominous turn. Whereas the forces of corporate culture have called for the application of business principles to the reorganization of higher education, many conservatives and liberals have adopted a much more radical agenda for public education. Central to this agenda is the attempt to transform public education from a public good, benefiting all students, to a private good designed to expand the profits of investors, educate students as consumers, and train young people for the low-paying jobs of the "New World Order." Although these three distinct projects address the meaning and purpose of public schools in different terms, they all work to undermine public education as a public entitlement, essential for the well-being of children and the future of democracy.

Privatization is the most powerful education reform movement and is funded by an array of conservative institutions, such as the Heritage Foundation, the

Hudson Institute, and the Olin Foundation.[36] Capitalizing on their wealth and media influence, these foundations have enlisted an army of conservative pundits, many of whom served in the Department of Education under Presidents Reagan and Bush. Some of the more well-known members of this reform movement include Chester Finn Jr., Lamar Alexander, Diane Ravitch, David Kearns, and William Bennett. Providing policy papers and op-ed commentaries, appearing on television talk shows, and running a variety of education clearinghouses and resource centers, these stalwart opponents of public education relentlessly blame the schools for the country's economic woes. Citing low test scores, a decline in basic skills, and the watering down of the school curriculum, Ravitch and others use such critiques to legitimate the ideology of privatization with its accompanying call for vouchers, privatized charter schools, and the placing of public schools entirely in the control of corporate contractors.[37] More specific reforms simply recycle right-wing ideological critiques calling for the replacement of teacher unions and "giving parents choice, back to-basics and performance-driven curriculums, management 'design teams' and accountability."[38]

Underlying the call for privatization is a reform movement in which public education is seen as "a local industry that over time will become a global business."[39] As a for-profit venture, public education represents a market worth more than $600 billion; and the importance of such a market has not been lost on conservatives, such as Chester Finn Jr. and David Kearns, both of whom have connections with for-profit schooling groups, such as the Edison Project and the North American Schools Development Corporation. At the level of policy, the right-wing assault has been quite successful. More than 28 states have drafted legislation supporting vouchers, choice programs, and contracting with for-profit management companies, such as the Edison Project and Sabin International Schools. But the public's perception of such ventures appears to be less enthusiastic, and rightly so. Many firms, such as Educational Alternatives Inc., which took over the Hartford and Baltimore public schools, have had their contracts canceled as a result of numerous public complaints. The complaints range from the way in which such firms deal with children with learning disabilities and engage in union busting to the charge that their cookie-cutter standardized curriculum and testing packages fail to provide the quality of education results that they initially promised.[40]

But there is more at stake in the privatization of public schooling than issues of public versus private ownership or public good versus private gain. There also is the issue of how individual achievement is weighed against issues of equity and the social good, how teaching and learning get defined, and what sorts of identities are produced when the histories, experiences, values, and desires of students are defined through corporate, rather than democratic, ideals.

Within the language of privatization and market reforms, there is a strong emphasis on standards, measurements of outcomes, and holding teachers and students more accountable. Privatization is an appealing prospect for legislators who do not want to spend money on schools and for those Americans who feel that they do not want to support public education through increased taxes. Such appeals are reductive in nature and hollow in substance. Not only do they abstract questions of equity and equality from the discourse of standards, they appropriate the democratic rhetoric of choice and freedom without addressing issues of power. Refusing to address the financial inequities that burden the public schools, the ideas and images that permeate this corporate model of schooling reek with the rhetoric of insincerity and the politics of social indifference. Jonathan Kozol captures this sentiment well. He insightfully writes:

> To speak of national standards and, increasingly, of national exams but never to dare speak of national equality is a transparent venture into punitive hypocrisy. Thus, the children in poor rural schools in Mississippi and Ohio will continue to get education funded at less than $4,000 yearly and children in the South Bronx will get less than $7,000, while children in the richest suburbs will continue to receive up to $18,000 yearly. But they'll all be told they must be held to the same standards and they'll all be judged, of course, by their performance on the same exams.[41]

Stripped of a language of social responsibility, the advocates of privatization reject the assumption that school failure might be better understood within the political, economic, and social dynamics of poverty, joblessness, sexism, race and class discrimination, unequal funding, or a diminished tax base. Rather, student failure, especially the failure of poor minority-group students, often is attributed to a genetically encoded lack of intelligence, a culture of deprivation, or simply pathology. Books such as *The Bell Curve*[42] and films such as *187* and *Dangerous Minds* reinforce such representations about African-American and Latino urban youth, as they perpetuate a history of racist exclusions. Similarly, such racist exclusions are being deepened by the informalities of privatization schemes in which schools simply mimic the free market, with the assumption that its regulatory and competitive spirit will allow the most motivated and gifted students to succeed. There is a shameful element of racism and a retrograde Social Darwinism that permeates this discourse, one that relinquishes the responsibility of parents, teachers, administrators, social workers, business people, and other members of the wider society to provide all young people with the cultural resources, economic opportunities, and social services necessary to learn without having to bear the crushing burdens of poverty, racism, and other forms of oppression.[43]

The excessive celebration of the sovereign interests of the individual does more than remove the dynamics of student performance from broader social and political considerations, it also feeds a value system in which compassion, solidarity, cooperation, social responsibility, and other attributes of education as a social good get displaced by defining education exclusively as a private good. If education is about, in part, the creating of particular identities, what is privileged in the corporate model is a notion of the student as an individual consumer and teachers as the ultimate salespeople.[44] David Labaree is right in arguing that such a model of education undermines the traditional notion that education is a public good that should benefit all children and be must be viewed as central to the democratic health of a society. But when viewed as a private good whose organizing principle is simply to mimic the market, education as the experience of democracy is transformed into a discourse and ideology of privilege driven by narrow individual interests. Labaree is quite clear on this issue:

> In an educational system where the consumer is king... Education ... is a private good that only benefits the owner, an investment in my future, not yours, in my children, not other people's children. For such an educational system to work effectively, it needs to focus a lot of attention on grading, sorting, and selecting students. It needs to provide a variety of ways for individuals to distinguish themselves from others — such as by placing themselves in a more prestigious college, a higher curriculum track, the top reading group, or the gifted program.[45]

Education in this framework becomes less a social investment than an individual investment, a vehicle for social mobility for those privileged to have the resources and power to make their choices matter, and a form of social constraint for those who lack such resources and for whom choice and accountability betray a legacy of broken promises and an ideology of bad faith.

The privatization model of schooling also defaults on the legacy of schooling as a public good by undermining the power of teachers to provide students with the vocabulary and skills of responsible citizenship. Under the drive to impose national curricula uniformity and standardized testing, privatizing school advocates devalue teacher authority and deskill teachers by dictating not only what they teach but also how they should teach. California, for example, is drafting legislation that mandates both the content of school knowledge and "more specific guidelines for when and how to teach various principles in the core subjects."[46] Teaching in this perspective is completely removed from the cultural and social contexts that shape particular traditions, histories, and experiences in a community and school. Hence there can be no recognition in this model of education reform that students come from different backgrounds, bring diverse cultural experiences, and relate to the world in different ways. There is no sense in this approach of what it means for teachers to make knowledge meaningful in order to make it critical and transformative. Pedagogical importance is no longer placed on having teachers begin with "where people are and how they actually live their lives."[47] Rather, teaching in the corporate model redefines importance by emphasizing the translation of educational exchange into financial exchange. Acknowledging students' histories, the stories that inform their lives, and weaving such information into webs of meaning that link the everyday with the academic is a powerful way to make knowledge meaningful; it also is an approach that cannot be standardized, routinized, and reduced to a prepackaged curriculum because it takes seriously the abilities of teachers to theorize, contextualize, and honor the diverse lives of their students.

A debilitating logic is at work in the corporate model of teaching with its mandated curriculum, top-down teaching practices, and national tests to measure education standards. Infused with the drive toward standardized curricula and teaching, "teachers and communities shorn of the capacity to use their own ideas, judgments, and initiative in matters of importance can't teach kids to do so."[48] Such pedagogical approaches have little to do with teaching responsible citizenship because they redefine teaching less as an intellectual activity and more as a depoliticized, deskilled clerkship. The main role of the teacher-turned-manager is to legitimate through mandated subject matter and pedagogical practices a market-based conception of the learner as simply a consumer of information. Yet such reforms have support, in spite of a long tradition of critique in the ways in which teachers are being deskilled and increasingly treated "more and more as impersonal instruments in a bureaucratic process than as thoughtful and creative intellectuals whose personal vision of education really matters."[49] Moreover, within the standardized teaching models proffered by corporations, it becomes difficult to offer students the opportunity to think critically about the knowledge they gain, to appreciate the value of learning as more than the mastery of discrete bits of information, or to learn to use knowledge as a form of power to fight substantive injustices in a market-based society founded on deep inequalities. Finally, it is no small matter that the project that fuels privatization not only celebrates competitive, self-interested individuals attempting to further their own needs and aspirations, it also takes place within a discourse of decline, a jeremiad against public life, and in doing so actually undermines the role that public schools might play in keeping the experiences, hopes, and dreams of a democracy alive for each successive generation of students.

While the discourse of privatization has as its major objective that public schools conform to the needs of the market and reflect more completely the interests of corporate culture, its goals are not limited to relocating the wholesale ownership and control of public schools to the private sector. This represents the most direct assault on schooling as a public sphere. A different, but no less important and dangerous strategy of the corporate dismantling and take over of public schools is the promotion of school choice, vouchers, and charters as ways of both opening public schools to private contractors and using public tax monies to finance the creation of private forms of education. Both approaches treat education as a private good, and both substitute the role of the student as a citizen for that of an education consumer. But the real danger at work in privatization, as Jeffrey Henig points out, is not simply that students who transfer into private schools will drain money from the public schools, but that they will further a process already at work in the larger society aimed at eroding "the public forums in which decisions with social consequences can be democratically resolved."[50]

The commercial logic that fuels this market-based reform movement also is evident in the way in which corporate culture targets schools not simply as investments for substantial profits, but also as training grounds for educating students to define themselves as consumers, rather than as multifaceted social actors. As schools struggle to raise money for texts, curricula, and extracurricular activities, they often find themselves engaging in partnerships with businesses that are all too willing either to provide free curriculum packages or, as in the case with Channel One, to provide each school with $50,000 in "free" electronic equipment, including VCRs, televisions, and satellite dishes — on the condition that the schools agree to broadcast a 10-minute program of current events and news material along with two minutes of commercials.[51]

The marriage of commercialism and pedagogy often takes place in schools with too few resources either to critically monitor how learning is structured or to recognize the sleight-of-hand that appears to be a generous offer on the part of corporations willing to provide curricula packages and rent school space. A couple of examples will suffice:

- In a recent cover story, *Business Week* reported on the adoption of a McDonald's-sponsored curriculum package by the Pembroke Lakes Elementary School in Broward County. Commenting on what one 10-year-old learned from the curriculum, *Business Week* claimed that "Travis Licate recently learned how to design a McDonald's restaurant, how a McDonald's works, and how to apply and interview for a job at McDonald's thanks to [the] seven-week company-sponsored class intended to teach kids about the work world."[52] When Travis was asked if the curriculum was worthwhile, he responded, "If you want to work in a McDonald's when you grow up, you already know what to do.... Also, McDonald's is better than Burger King."[53]

- According to the Center for Commercial-Free Public Education, Exxon developed a curriculum that teaches young students that the Valdez oil spill was an example of environmental protection. The center also cites a Nike-sponsored curriculum that teaches students to learn the cycle of a Nike shoe but fails to address "the sweatshop portion of the manufacturing process."[54]

Such curricula have little to do with critical learning and a great deal to do with shaping students' identities, dreams, and desires within the limited and debilitating image of preparing for work and life in the fast-food and service industries.

- Caught in a financial crunch, many school systems not only accept corporate-sponsored curricula but also lease space in their hallways, on their buses, and even on book covers. Cover Concepts Marketing Services Inc., for example, provides schools with free book covers strategically designed to promote brand-name products that include Nike, Gitano, FootLocker, Starburst, Nestle, and Pepsi. The covers are distributed to more than 8,000 public schools and reach an audience of some six million high school, junior high, and elementary school students.[55]

- In Colorado Springs, Palmer High School allows Burger King and Sprite to advertise on the sides of its school buses. In Salt Lake City, Youthtalk Advertising Agency places acrylic-faced advertising billboards in school restrooms and cafeterias. It is estimated by the company that more than "80,000 students are exposed to the ads while standing at urinals and sitting in toilet stalls."[56]

In this instance, schools are transformed into commercial spheres while their role as public spheres is undermined, if not discarded, and students become subject to the whims and practices of marketers whose agenda has nothing to do with critical learning and a great deal to do with restructuring civic life in the image of market culture.[57]

Civic courage as a defining principle of civil society in this context is utterly devalued as corporate power transforms school knowledge, such that students are taught to recognize brand names or learn the appropriate attitudes for future work in low-skilled, low-paying jobs. What they are no longer taught is how to connect the meaning of work to the imperatives of a strong democracy. What links Channel One, Nike, Pepsi, the Campbell Soup Company, the McDonald's Corporation, and a host of other corporations is that they substitute corporate propaganda for real learning, upset the requisite balance between the public and the private, and in so doing treat schools as if they were like any other business.

Underlying the attempt to redefine the meaning and purpose of schooling as part of a market economy, rather than a fundamental feature of substantive democracy, is a model of society in which "consumer accountability [is] mediated by a relationship with an educational market [rather than] a democratic accountability mediated by a relationship with the whole community of citizens."[58] Most disturbing about the market approach to schooling is that it contains no special consideration for the vocabulary of ethics and values. British educator, Gerald Grace, is right on target in warning that when public education becomes a venue for making a profit, delivering a product, or constructing consuming subjects, education reneges on its responsibilities for creating a democracy of citizens by shifting its focus on producing a democracy of consumers.[59] The corporate model of schooling and the market culture it legitimates undermine the traditional notion that schools are the most visible symbols we have for educating students in the skills of leadership, citizenship, and democracy. Couched in the language of business competition and individual success, the current education reform movement must be recognized as a full-fledged attack on both public education and democracy itself. David Stratman's warning that the goal of such a movement "is not to raise the expectations of our young people but to narrow, stifle, and crush them"[60] needs to be taken seriously by anyone concerned about public education and the fundamental role it should play in placing limits on market culture, affirming the language of moral compassion, and expanding the meaning of freedom and choice to broader considerations of equity, justice, and social responsibility.

Education and the Imperatives of Democracy

I want to return to an issue I raised in the beginning of this fastback, when I argued that corporations have been given too much power in this society and hence the need for educators and others to address the threat this poses to all facets of public life organized around the non-commodified principles of justice, freedom, and equality. Challenging the encroachment of corporate power is essential if democracy is to remain a defining principle of education and everyday life. Part of such a challenge necessitates that educators and others create organizations capable of mobilizing civic dialogue, provide an alternative conception of the meaning and purpose of higher and public education, and move political organizations toward producing legislation to challenge corporate power's ascendancy over the institutions and mechanisms of civil society. This project means that educators, students, and others will have to provide the rationale and mobilize the possibility for creating enclaves of resistance, new public cultures for collective development, and institutional spaces that highlight, nourish, and evaluate the tension between civil society and corporate power while simultaneously struggling to prioritize citizen rights over consumer rights.

In strategic terms, revitalizing public dialogue suggests that educators need to take seriously the importance of defending higher and public education as institutions of civic culture whose purpose is to educate students for active citizenship.[61] Situated within a broader context of issues concerned with social responsibility, politics, and the dignity of human life, schooling should be defended as a site that offers students the opportunity to involve themselves in the deepest problems of society, to acquire the knowledge, skills, and ethical vocabulary necessary for what Václav Havel calls "the richest possible participation in public life."[62] Educators need to come together to defend schools as indispensable to the life of the nation because they are one of the few public spaces left where students can learn the power of and engage in the experience of democracy. In the face of corporate takeovers, the ongoing commodification of the curriculum, and the turning of students into consumers, such a project requires educators to mount a collective struggle to reassert the crucial importance of higher and public education in offering students the skills they need for learning how to govern, taking risks, and developing the knowledge necessary for deliberation, reasoned arguments, and social action. At issue here is providing students with an education that allows them to recognize the dream and promise of a substantive democracy, particularly the idea that as citizens they are "entitled to public services, decent housing, safety, security, support during hard times, and most importantly, some power over decision making."[63] Carol Ascher, Norm Fruchter, and Robert Berne capture the gravity of such a project in their claim that,

> the urgency to solve the inequities in schooling is perhaps the most important reason for continuing the struggle to reform public education. For we will not survive as a republic nor move toward a genuine democracy unless we can narrow the gap between the rich and the poor, reduce our racial and ethnic divides, and create a deeper sense of community.[64]

But more is needed than defending higher and public education as central to developing and nourishing the proper balance between democratic public spheres and commercial power, between identities founded on democratic principles and identities steeped in forms of competitive, self-interested individualism that celebrate their own material and ideological advantages. Given the current assault on educators at all levels of schooling, it is politically crucial that teachers be defended as public intellectuals who provide an indispensable service to the nation. Such an appeal cannot be made merely in the name of professionalism but in terms of the civic duty such intellectuals provide. Intellectuals who inhabit our nation's schools represent the conscience of a society, in part, because they shape the conditions under which future generations learn about themselves and their relations to others and the world, but also because they engage pedagogical practices that are political, rather than simply technical. At their best such pedagogical practices bear witness to the ethical and political dilemmas that animate the broader social landscape.

Organizing against the corporate takeover of schools also suggests, especially within higher education, fighting to protect the jobs of full-time faculty, turning adjunct jobs into full-time positions, expanding benefits to part-time workers, and putting power into the hands of faculty and students. Moreover, such a struggle must address the exploitative conditions under which many graduate students work, constituting a de facto army of service workers who are underpaid, overworked, and shorn of any real power or benefits.[65] Similarly, educators at the public school levels are under massive assault in this country. Not only are they increasingly losing their autonomy for context-specific teaching, but also they increasingly bear the burden, especially in the urban centers, of overcrowded classes, limited resources, and hostile legislators. Such educators need to join with community people, social movements, and academics in higher education to found a common platform that resists the corporatizing of schools, the deskilling of teachers, and the hiring of untrained teachers to assume classroom responsibilities. Resisting the corporate takeover of schools also suggests that public school educators fight to protect collective bargaining, to strengthen health benefits for teachers, and to put more power into the hands of faculty, parents, and students.

In the face of the growing corporatization of schools, progressive educators at all levels of education also should organize to challenge commodified forms of learning in the public schools. This suggests producing and distributing resources that educate teachers and students to the dangers of a corporate ethos that simply treats schools as extensions of the marketplace and students as potential consumers. At the level of policy, advertising, merchandizing, and commercial interests should be banned from the public schools; and educators should establish a bill of rights identifying and outlining the range of noncommercial relations that can be used to mediate between the public schools, higher education, and the business world. If the forces of corporate culture are to be challenged, progressive educators also must enlist the help of diverse communities, local and federal government, and other political forces to ensure that public schools are adequately funded so that they will not have to rely on corporate sponsorship and advertising revenues. How public schools educate youth for the future will determine the meaning and substance of democracy itself. Such a responsibility necessitates giving priority to democratic community, citizen rights, and the public good over market relations, narrow consumer demands, and corporate interests.

The corporatizing of American education reflects a crisis of vision regarding the meaning and purpose of democracy at a time when "market cultures, market moralities, market mentalities [are] shattering community, eroding civic society, [and] undermining the nurturing system for children."[66] Yet such a crisis also represents a unique opportunity for progressive educators to expand and deepen the meaning of democracy — radically defined as a struggle to combine the distribution of wealth, income, and knowledge with a recognition and positive valorizing of cultural diversity — by reasserting the primacy of politics, power, and struggle as a pedagogical task.[67] Educators need to confront the march of corporate power by resurrecting a noble tradition, extending from Horace Mann to Martin Luther King Jr., in which education is affirmed as a political process that encourages people to identify themselves as more than consuming subjects and democracy as more than a spectacle of market culture.

Notes

1. W.E.B. Du Bois, *Color and Democracy: Colonies and Peace* (Milwood, N.Y.: Kraus-Thomson, 1975), pp. 99, 142.
2. The advertisement appears in *World Traveler* (March 1998), p. 76.
3. Francis Fukuyama, *The End of History and the Last Man* (New York: Free Press, 1989).
4. Seyla Benhabib, "The Democratic Moment and the Problem of Difference," in *Democracy and Difference*, edited by Seyla Benhabib (Princeton: Princeton University Press, 1996), p. 9.
5. Francis Fukuyama, "The End of History," *The National Interest* (Summer 1989), p. 2.
6. Stuart Ewen has traced this trend historically to the emergence in the 19th century of the culture of abundance, which allowed "for the flowering of a provocative, if somewhat passive, conception of democracy.... consumer democracy." See Stuart Ewen, *All Consuming Images* (New York: Basic Books, 1988), p. 12.
7. The classic dominant texts on corporate culture are Terrance Deal and Alan Kennedy, *Corporate Culture: The Rites and Rituals of Corporate Life* (Reading, Mass.: Addison-Wesley, 1982), and Thomas Peterson and Robert Waterman, *In Search of Excellence* (New York: Harper & Row, 1982). I also want to point out that cor-

porate culture is a dynamic, ever-changing force. But in spite of its innovations and changes, it rarely, if ever, challenges the centrality of the profit motive or fails to prioritize commercial considerations over a set of values that would call the class-based system of capitalism into question. For a brilliant discussion of the changing nature of corporate culture in light of the cultural revolution of the 1960s, see Thomas Frank, *The Conquest of Cool* (Chicago: University of Chicago Press, 1997).

8. Alan Bryman, *Disney and His Worlds* (New York: Routledge, 1995), p. 154.

9. There are many books that address this issue, but one of the most helpful in providing hard statistical evidence for the growing corporate monopolization of American society can be found in Dan Hazen and Julie Winokur, eds., *We the Media* (New York: New Press, 1997). See also, Robert W. McChesney, *Corporate Media and the Threat to Democracy* (New York: Seven Stories Press, 1997); and Erik Barneouw et al., *Conglomerates and the Media* (New York: New Press, 1997).

10. Robin D.G. Kelley, *Yo' Mama's Disfunktional: Fighting the Culture Wars in Urban America* (Boston: Beacon Press, 1997).

11. Peter Edelman, "The Worst Thing Bill Clinton Has Done," *Atlantic Monthly* (March 1997): 43-58.

12. For a context from which to judge the effects of such cuts on the poor and children of America, see Children's Defense Fund, *The State of America's Children: Yearbook 1997* (Washington, D.C., 1977).

13. Cited in Ruth Sidel, *Keeping Women and Children Last* (New York: Penguin, 1996), p. xiv.

14. See for example, Paul Baran and Paul M. Sweezy, *Monopoly Capital* (New York: Monthly Review Press, 1966).

15. See especially, John Dewey, *Democracy and Education* (New York: Free Press, 1944, originally published in 1916).
16. Cited in Stanley Aronowitz, "The New Corporate University," *Dollars and Sense* (March/April 1998): 32.
17. Critical educators have provided a rich history of how public and higher education have been shaped by the politics, ideologies, and images of industry. For example, see Samuel Bowles and Herbert Gintis, *Schooling in Capitalist America* (New York: Basic Books, 1976); Michael Apple, *Ideology and Curriculum* (New York: Routledge, 1977); Martin Carnoy and Henry Levin, *Schooling and Work in the Democratic State* (Stanford, Calif.: Stanford University Press, 1985); Stanley Aronowitz and Henry A. Giroux, *Education Still Under Siege* (Westport, Conn.: Bergin and Garvey, 1993); Dennis Carlson, *Education and Culture in New Times* (New York: Teachers College Press, 1997).
18. Katherine S. Mangan, "Corporate Know-How Lands Presidencies for a Growing Number of Business Deans," *Chronicle of Higher Education*, 27 March 1998, p. A43.
19. Ibid., p. A44.
20. Stanley Aronowitz, "The New Corporate University," *Dollars and Sense* (March/April 1998): 32-35.
21. Louis V. Gerstner Jr., "Public Schools Need to Go the Way of Business," *USA Today*, 4 March 1998, p. 13A.
22. Ibid.
23. Catherine. S. Manegold, "Study Says Schools Must Stress Academics," *New York Times*, 23 September 1998, p. A22. It is difficult to understand how any school system could have subjected students to such a crude lesson in commercial pedagogy.
24. Stanley Aronowitz and William De Fazio, "The New Knowledge Work," in *Education: Culture, Economy,*

Society, edited by A.H. Halsey, Hugh Lauder, Phillip Brown, and Amy Stuart Wells (New York: Oxford University Press, 1997), p. 193.

25. This is amply documented in Jeremy Rifkin, *The End of Work* (New York: G.P. Putnam's Sons, 1995); William Wolman and Anne Colamosca, *The Judas Economy: The Triumph of Capital and the Betrayal of Work* (Reading, Mass.: Addison-Wesley, 1997); Stanley Aronowitz and William DiFazio, *The Jobless Future* (Minneapolis: University of Minnesota Press, 1994); *The New York Times Report: The Downsizing of America* (New York: Times Books, 1996); Stanley Aronowitz and Jonathan Cutler, *Post-Work* (New York: Routledge, 1998).

26. Ralph Nader, "Civil Society and Corporate Responsibility," Speech given to the National Press Club and broadcast on C-Span2 on 25 March 1998.

27. Cornel West, "The New Cultural Politics of Difference," *October* 53 (Summer 1990): 35.

28. Katherine S. Mangan, op. cit., p. A44.

29. Carlin cited in William H. Honan, "The Ivory Tower Under Siege," *New York Times*, 4 January 1998, Section 4A, p. 33.

30. Ibid.

31. Cited in Bill Tierney, "Tenure and Community in Academe," *Educational Researcher* 26 (November 1997): 17.

32. Alison Schneider, "More Professors Are Working Part Time, and More Teach at 2-Year Colleges," *Chronicle of Higher Education*, 13 March 1998, p. A14.

33. Eaton's salary was cited in "GMC CEO PAY," *USA Today*, 21 April 1998, p. 1B. Reference to Eisner, cited in Liane Bonin, "Tragic Kingdom," *Detour Magazine* (April 1998): 70.

34. Stanley Aronowitz, "The Corporate University," *Dollars and Sense* (March/April 1998): 34-35.

35. This issue is taken up in Michael Berube, "Why Inefficiency Is Good for Universities," *Chronicle of Higher Education*, 27 March 1998, pp. B4-B5.
36. Phyllis Vine, "To Market, To Market," *The Nation*, 8/15 September 1997, pp. 11-17.
37. Many of these reports are produced by right-wing think tanks with a vested interest in the privatization movement. For example, see Paul Pekin, "Schoolhouse Crock: Right-Wing Myths Behind the 'New Stupidity'," *Extra!* (January/February 1998): 9-10. For an excellent rebuttal of the charge that American public education is in a state of disastrous decline, see David Berliner and Bruce Biddle, *The Manufactured Crisis* (Reading, Mass.: Addison-Wesley, 1995); Gerald Bracey, "What Happened to America's Public Schools? Not What You Think?" *American Heritage* (November 1997): 39-52.
38. Cited in Vine, op. cit., p. 12.
39. Cited in Vine, ibid., p. 11.
40. For a summary of the historical failures of privatization, see Carol Ascher, Norm Fruchter, and Robert Berne, *Hard Lessons: Public Schools and Privatization* (New York: Twentieth Century Fund, 1996). For a specific analysis of the failure of Education Alternatives Inc. in Baltimore and Hartford, see Alex Molnar, *Giving Kids the Business* (Boulder, Colo.: Westview, 1996), especially chapter 4, "Schools for Profit," pp. 77-116. Also, see Phyllis Vine, "To Market, To Market," *The Nation*, 8/15 September 1987, pp. 11-17; Bruce Shapiro, "Privateers Flunk Schools," *The Nation*, 19 February 1998, p. 4.
41. Jonathan Kozol, "Saving Public Education," *The Nation*, 17 February 1997, p. 16.
42. Richard J. Herrnstein and Charles Murray, *The Bell Curve* (New York: Free Press, 1994).

43. For a vivid and compassionate examination of how these conditions limit the opportunities for students to get a decent education, see Jonathan Kozol, *Amazing Grace* (New York: Crown, 1995). For a more specific analysis of the relationship between racism, poverty, and schools, see James Comer, *Waiting for a Miracle: Why Schools Can't Solve Our Problems — And How We Can* (New York: Dutton, 1997).
44. This is particularly true when schools engage in market-sponsored contests in which teachers spend valuable teaching time coaching kids how to collect cash receipts, sell goods to their friends and neighbors, or learn the rules for bringing in profits for companies who then offer prizes to schools. See Alex Molnar, *Giving Kids the Business* (Boulder, Colo.: Westview, 1996), especially chapter 3.
45. David Labaree, "Are Students 'Consumers'?" *Education Week*, 17 September 1997, p. 48.
46. Kathleen Kennedy Manzo, "California School Board Infusing Pedagogy into Frameworks," *Education Week*, 11 March 1998, p. 7.
47. Lawrence Grossberg, *Bringing It All Back Home: Essays on Cultural Studies* (Durham, N.C.: Duke University Press, 1997), p. 257.
48. Deborah W. Meier, "Saving Public Education," *The Nation*, 17 February 1997, p. 24.
49. Svi Shapiro, "Public School Reform: The Mismeasure of Education," *Tikkun* 13 (Winter 1998): 54. See also, Henry A. Giroux, *Teachers as Intellectuals* (Westport, Conn.: Bergin and Garvey, 1988); Stanley Aronowitz and Henry A. Giroux, *Education Still Under Siege* (Westport, Conn.: Bergin and Garvey, 1993).

50. Jeffrey Henig, "The Danger of Market Rhetoric," in *Selling Out Our Schools*, edited by Robert Lowe and Barbara Miner (Milwaukee: Rethinking Schools Institute, 1996), p. 11. See also, Jeffrey Henig, *Rethinking School Choice* (Princeton, N.J.: Princeton University Press, 1994).
51. For a sustained critique of Channel One, see Henry A. Giroux, *Disturbing Pleasures: Learning Popular Culture* (New York: Routledge, 1994).
52. Cover story, "This Lesson Is Brought to You By," *Business Week*, 30 June 1997, p. 69.
53. Ibid.
54. Cited in "Reading, Writing . . . and Purchasing," *Educational Leadership* 56, no. 2 (1998): 16.
55. Consumer Union Education Services, *Captive Kids: A Report on Commercial Pressures on Kids at School* (Yonkers, N.Y., 1998), p. 9.
56. Ibid., p. 26.
57. This issue is taken up in great detail in Alex Molnar, op. cit. For a more general analysis of the relationship between corporate culture and schooling, see Joe Kincheloe and Shirley Steinberg, eds., *KinderCulture: The Corporate Construction of Childhood* (Boulder, Colo.: Westview, 1997).
58. Gerald Grace, "Politics, Markets, and Democratic Schools: On the Transformation of School Leadership," in *Education: Culture, Economy, Society*, edited by A.H. Halsey, Hugh Lauder, Phillip Brown, and Amy Stuart Wells (New York: Oxford University Press, 1997), p. 314.
59. Gerald Grace, op. cit., p. 315.
60. David Stratman, "School Reform and the Attack on Public Education," *Dollars and Sense* (March/April 1988): 7.
61. There are a number of books that take up the relationship between schooling and democracy. Some of the more im-

portant recent critical contributions include: Elizabeth A. Kelly, *Education, Democracy, & Public Knowledge* (Boulder, Colo.: Westview, 1995); Wilfred Carr and Anthony Hartnett, *Education and the Struggle for Democracy* (Philadelphia: Open University Press, 1996); David T. Sehr, *Education for Public Democracy* (Albany: State University of New York Press, 1997); James Fraser, *Reading, Writing and Justice: School Reform as If Democracy Matters* (Albany: State University of New York Press, 1997); see also, Henry A. Giroux, *Schooling and the Struggle for Public Life* (Minneapolis: University of Minnesota Press, 1988), and Henry A. Giroux, *Pedagogy and the Politics of Hope* (Boulder, Colo.: Westview, 1997).

62. Václav Havel, "The State of the Republic," *New York Review of Books*, 22 June 1998, p. 45.
63. Robin D.G. Kelley, "Neo-Cons of the Black Nation," *Black Renaissance Noire* 1 (Summer/Fall 1997): 146.
64. Carol Ascher, Norm Fruchter, and Robert Berne, *Hard Lessons: Public Schools and Privatization* (New York: Twentieth Century Fund, 1996), p. 112.
65. See Cary Nelson, ed., *Will Teach for Food: Academic Labor in Crisis* (Minneapolis: University of Minnesota Press, 1997).
66. Cornel West, "America's Three-Fold Crisis," *Tikkun* 9, no. 2 (1994): 42.
67. On this issue, see Nancy Fraser, *Justice Interruptus* (New York: Routledge, 1997).